LETTERS FROM LIMBO

Letters
from
Limbo

Jeanne Marie Beaumont

CavanKerry ❖ Press LTD.

CavanKerry Press Ltd.
Fort Lee, New Jersey
www.cavankerrypress.org

Publisher's Cataloging-in-Publication
(Provided by Quality Books, Inc.)

    Beaumont, Jeanne Marie, author.
      [Poems. Selections]
      Letters from limbo / Jeanne Marie Beaumont.—First
    edition.
      pages cm
      ISBN 978-1-933880-59-4

      1. American poetry. 2. Poetry. I. Title.

PS3552.E2318A6 2016   811'.54
            QBI16-1118

Cover artwork *Grasp Reality* © Ben Seidelman
Cover and interior text design by Ryan Scheife, Mayfly Design
First Edition 2016, Printed in the United States of America

NOTABLE VOICES
CavanKerry ⊛ Press

CavanKerry Press is proud to publish the works of
established poets of merit and distinction.

Discover
JERSEY
ARTS

NEW JERSEY
STATE COUNCIL
ON THE ARTS

CavanKerry Press is grateful for the support it receives
from the New Jersey State Council on the Arts.

ALSO BY JEANNE MARIE BEAUMONT

POETRY

Placebo Effects (1997)
Curious Conduct (2004)
Burning of the Three Fires (2010)

ANTHOLOGY

The Poets' Grimm: 20th Century Poems from Grimm Fairy Tales
(co-edited with Claudia Carlson, 2003)

Contents

CROSSING

ASYLUM SONG

HOLDING

LETTERS
FROM
LIMBO

limbo . . . 1. Often **Limbo.** *Theology.* The abode of just or innocent souls excluded from the beatific vision but not condemned to further punishment. **2.** A region or condition of oblivion or neglect: *Management kept her promotion in limbo for months.* **3.** A state or place of confinement. **4.** An intermediate place or state. (from *The American Heritage Dictionary*)

*

A church decision to abolish limbo has long been expected. Benedict and his predecessor, the late Pope John Paul II, expressed misgivings about the concept. Benedict, when he was still Cardinal Joseph Ratzinger and the church's top enforcer of dogma, said he viewed limbo as a mere "theological hypothesis." Never part of formal doctrine because it does not appear in Scripture, limbo was removed from the Catholic catechism 15 years ago. (from *Los Angeles Times,* April 21, 2007)

CROSSING

Crossing

In a city that was not my own I crossed
a bridge over the river and wandered a long while.
Later, I crossed another flowers had been
woven around. Something was going on today
in the city. It rained. Stopped raining. Rained again.
I found a gallery of lost women, their dresses shrunk
to doll-size, their non-names engraved on plaques.
Leaning over my coffee, I listened as story led to
story. I bought a movie ticket and waited in a red seat
for the feature presentation. In the film a woman
set herself afire. Two patrons walked out. After,
I browsed spices and baking supplies—enticing
but I didn't bite. I crossed the river and searched
through moldering books in a back room. I viewed
an ancient scroll that stretched for yards, each episode
rolling to the next. I knew the city was a repository
I had only begun to tap. I knew the bridges sutured
the river, that I kept crossing between the dead and
the living. Much digging was underway. I recalled
the phrase from an old tale predicting *the bright sun
will bring it to light.* Walkers every day tamped down
with their feet what squirmed again to the surface
demanding to be recognized. One day of wandering
was coming to an end. It was the inescapable labor
of time—the city would unearth my secret name
and soon be summoning me back. When my cup
was served, a heart steamed toward me from the foam.

Letter from Limbo

If it proves possible, could you please send replacement
Victrola needles (tungsten), an atlas of your world (recent),
and a box of tailor's chalk? Also, bishops for chess sets
(light and dark); they disappear at an alarming rate.
And, if it's not imposing too much, some small
thing salvaged from the sea, even a piece of shell
or driftwood, that retains a scent of salt and scales.
Don't think me monstrous for mentioning it, but
might you enclose a so-called rabbit's foot?—
not for luck of course, that issue's long moot—
it's just that I so miss something soft at hand to pet.
I wouldn't inconvenience you for all of heaven's grails;
any item that's too much bother above, I beg you *forget*.

Letter from Limbo

How often our locale is misunderstood, e.g.,
Management kept her promotion in limbo for months.
Our limits of patience fortunately are longer-winded.
Months? Hah! I live among the lineaments of
Calm faces, limpid glances that linger but will not leer.
We do not loiter in lingerie, nor are we lotus-eaters,
Logy and lorn, unbecomingly attached to our lounges.
We are not lazy in the least.
Who arrives limping or lisping is soon limber, loquacious.
The lowest lummox soon lithe and lucid.
We have no use for litigators or locks.
Yes, our Library is full of the unfinished, the labeled
On hold, the left to languish.
Lovely films that never saw the light of your days
Are released here and delight us. Our weakness for
Lengthy lullabies is not as loony as it sounds.
We have a low-key liturgy that is voluntary and ludic.
Planned luminescence, you might say, or I will.
A blessed longanimity purrs like a limo and
Lionizes every supple soul, leaving each
Limboling lustrous under our peculiar limelight.

Yet

I knew from an early time.
Not born yet,
no crib yet.

Not reading yet, yet drawing.
Not yet old enough to ...
yet wanting to.

Forbidden yet inviting.
You can't go in yet.
You can't leave yet.

Yet pushed me back, yet
held me close.
I wasn't there yet

I was afraid. Yet made
a fearsome aid. Yet kind.
No one's yet died.

Should I ...? No, *ne, nyet,* not yet.
So much I didn't know yet.
But yet I understood.

The Room and the View

(after Bonnard's *Dining Room on the Garden*)

Light delivers a message these subjects absorb faithfully.
This nun of a white pitcher, monk-brown sugar bowl—
A tablecloth cloisters. A V-shaped vase offers red prayers,
Paired compotes compare visions, two small bowls lean to
Meditate or beg. Each has made its vow of silence.
The window holds a garden scene, split like a diptych or
Japanese screen, divided also by color: blue | green.

Nothing here beckons to me, no thing needs my attention.
Why then do I long to live here, to fall into the painting,
To follow the path my eyes blaze and allow the lush
Pigments to enwrap me like expensive scarves?
The woman hiding behind the flowers is not my mother.
She will not welcome me, or anyone. I may not be
Permitted to use a chair. Perhaps I am already there—

That ghost streak melting its gold into the wall.
There seems no other way out. There is scant air.
For many years I kept to a room I could not bear
To exit, the world beyond the window baffling, unreachable
As Mars. The room is thick with bars, I see that now,
Camouflaged by décor, by window frame, by fabric—
I can't see how to get past all these verticals.

Must all rooms resemble this one, a show of comforts
That sets a snare? No, art is blessed illusion, and
This square canvas composed to conjure dimension.
Such bright fruit will not give bite, nor milk-white pitcher sour.
How close to transcendence the whole scene wavers!
For here is the light of a mind, bold and incendiary.
The object in mind is oil. No room but color.

A Day in Lavender

At the circus there was never enough lavender. Later, at the gallery, some stains of the recently departed. I spoke of the syringe as an object at which it is terrible to look. No, you said, in the painting it is a subject, with a hint of lavender. We'd passed a bicycle, its frame slightly bent up but undeniably a shade of lavender. Somewhat like a giant's eyeglasses, I said, having a fondness for frames and what one sees in them. Had I ever owned a lavender bicycle? My childhood bedroom was painted lavender, and I recall a stuffed chair with lavender flowers. My great aunt's bedroom was also lavender and so was her bath, *entirely.* Towels? you asked. I nodded. And even the soap. Now *here,* you pointed out hours later, a delicate and somber lavender tinting the late evening sky, is a woman adrift on a bed, a possible subject posed for our appraisal. But no, I said, in the painting she becomes an object, with a hint of lavender. You must have loved her a lot, you said. Then night swiped our color away.

Blue Sister Blues

Ten toes, blueberries ripe for plucking,
  violets bloomed through your limbs like a bruise,
nearly Easter the year you dropped in,
  your bud-sized heart born confused,
                heart born confused.

Ten days in our tree top you spent rocking,
  wound in the blanket of your virgin name,
borne in the pink limbo of our imagining,
  where you curl a pilot's blue flame,
                pilot's blue flame.

Ten years from brother to me where you're missing.
  Released into air, bluebird, how you fly,
refusing to land, refusing to home
  till we lose you against the blue sky,
                against the blue sky.

Letter from Limbo

Now that our version of a spring thaw's arrived,
the ground's even spongier than usual. We wear
waders and waddle mightily out through the muck
and back, out and back, out and back,
endurance a sure cause for civic pride,
were it not futile for us to claim virtue.

You may have heard of the decertifying of our
pitiable province? Apparently the doctrine of Limbo
in the 21st century was an encumbrance, that or
mere redundancy. All the unbaptized babies
have grown. Limbo's grayer than last week's gravy.
Nothing's cute about our inhabitants, but please
twitch with the surety we're not to be disappeared
or discontinued; we're not railroads or coal stoves.

Each morning the agony returns afresh:
we're stuck. Want a rewrite? We're staying.
Our cobblers and horologists labor on.
Only our post office has been officially closed,
Zip code annulled, addresses obliterated.
As ever, we wait to be delivered . . .

Letter from Limbo

We call this *wind-shifting time*, when the fires
from the land beyond our border conspire
with unfavorable currents to turn up our heat.
The ground's grown sere and bumpy, yet
we stumble much across it, our waders abandoned.
Each soul quivers, makes its own mirage pool on
the parched road. This is no punishment, no more
excruciating than the aeons or hours on hold here.

In fact, a sort of tropical languor ensues.
I can't escape the something-I-forgot-to-do
sense, that *what* that slinks over the mind's
ledge, sinks out of reach. Water fount? Inscribe
belief? While we don't covet our infernal neighbor's
sulfurous stench, against which our olfactories
have been granted sturdy shields, we envy,
in this sultry season, their plethora of shades.

Letter from Limbo

If you'd stop to imagine
us (would you?), you might picture us hung suspended
in icicle-like pods

and true, our longest, lonest
season finds us encased like twigs or wires after an ice storm
though some believe it's tears

of seraphim that befall us
and some those of saints, I'm skeptical such far agencies
would weather us so.

These stretches of stasis
we endure like a cryogenics of the soul, yet feel no chill.
Immobilized yet not discomforted,

we are as beetles in amber
or like bristles caught within the canvas's encaustic.
We call ourselves working stills.

Or like the ones in fairytales
who slumbered under glass or up in brambled towers.
(In trying to explain what we're like

I feel the trap of metaphor itself.)
It's almost a miracle the way the ground's stalagmites
don't pierce our feet—did we

live right enough for one mercy?
And there's a glistening in the figurations of hoarfrost that
near-halos our stalled society

as close as we get to a notion
of "heavenly." How beatific we appear in our sheaths.
It's then we truly inhabit this place:

the prolonged passage when each
realization stops creeping and, yielding to the lure of stalemate,
crystallizes—like ... like   nothing

Folk Art Portraits of the 1700s

Facing the faces.
        The silences.
The stern past
        there's no turning from—
      the bird on the finger perch   meets each eye—
how does one keep
a straight face?
        A can-do candor,
no nonsense, no pretense—
        the children even more somber still.

Bare-boned holdings
        small book, bent flower, folded fan,
a pen (for a man),
        one hand in the hand of another
or covering one's own hand,
        a child's shoe,
some red around it like an underthought
      as though blood let out and—what can one do?—
was paint-stanched
        hogging the pigment.
        The eye goes right to it.

Oil this deaf artist's usual medium
though in one exceptional
mourning picture
                    a man walks with the aid
of crutches
              finely embroidered in gold silk—
the eye's drawn there too—under the glass—

minute gilt stitches—
                        and three centuries pass

Fifteen Views of a Christening Gown

That it was fine linen flawlessly stitched,
        as silken as new skin.

That it was the color of ivory or an old book's pages
        left blank in the front.

In the beginning shape of the letter A, it made
        a long A sound. With lace.

Because she was heard to say it had been passed
        down. *Saved.* This was not the first.

That it draped abundantly, way way past
        the babe's curled-in feet.

That it contained. And it concealed.

As a sacramental dress, it too had been blessed.

That it came with a matching hat, beribboned.

That it was closed with the agitations of pearls,
        buttons aglow like infant nails.

That it was a small bride. Something borrowed
        that embraced something blue.

That it smelled as clean as God.

April it was. A long long aching shape.

Because she could not forget, they remembered.

That it was the last. Not first.

Because she was heard to say, *we buried her in it.*

In Preparation

(after Gustave Courbet)

Save me—I'm caught in a net of quandary.
No sooner am I dressed than I am being taken
out of my clothes. Or are they helping me
into them? It appears I am being attired
for marriage, one of death's deft hands.

Around me a clutch of women painted stuck like doors:
forever two hoist a sheet (some say a shroud),
one is drying or bathing my feet, another
brings a tureen to the table, or is she removing it?
The problem is art's, but I'm in the midst.

Stockings, victuals, so-called shroud—all for me?
These women, are they what I was, what I will be?
Am I victim? Being prepped to be gazed at?
For some prone position? For a *him*?
Help me. It appears I can't go forward or

backward. I'm awkward. Unfinished. I hold
a mirror as though approaching a gorgon,
a mirror that only I can look in. I have heard
the dead cannot face mirrors, nor can
the dead keep a mirror up. There. Breath.

I fog it with my breath. Oh, what is this sound—
stiff brushes turning into baffled hisses ...
how my depiction's deemed "mysterious." But isn't
everyone's? This miss tells two sure things: I'm to be wed.
My paint is drying. Guess whether I am dead or dying.

Letter from Limbo

It can be claimed of almost
all who abide here—who are
      after all the just—
that we would bend
over backwards, go
      far out on a limb to do
what any righteous friend
should do.
      True, we tend
to be more limber
during our thaw time, quicker
      to remember
what our mutual duties entail.
But eventually we prevail
      whatever the seasonal hindrance.
Despite our recent dis-
membering (yet too fresh a cut
      to write without a wince)
we believe we still flicker
about the cosmic edges, tingle
      as God's phantom limb . . .
there   or not there
      here
we are, accommodating as noodles
whether you raise—
      or lower—the bar.

Dearest Limboling,

Thank you for seasons,
vivid atmosphere.
I admire the
calm way you endure
what seems an ordeal.
Have you any name?
Can you locate souls
(may need a favor)?
Would blackboard chalk work?
Could you carve woodblocks
into crude bishops?
For needle request
I'll need to consult
the collectibles
and antiques market—
begging your patience,
I'm afraid the world
has utterly changed.
(See atlas enclosed.)

Letter from Limbo

Let this missive assure you, except for
a recurrent shortage of pronouns, nothing
and no one tortures our inhabitants.
Odd habits, yes, admittedly. A body got
framed in wire and failure but was not *caged*.
Another was discovered draped in rosaries,
but in no circles is serendipity of this sort
considered a sin. Irony is not inescapable.
The words *menial* and *tedium* often float
too handily among the implements, and
the word *temporarily* endures as a favorite joke.
Some like their tee-shirts soaked in tea,
like memories, the effect a sepia tie-dyed stain,
but it doesn't sink in *too* deep. Absurdity only
threatens to take over without ever doing so.
And paper images remain merely paper.
The daily news can reliably be rolled
into a thinking cap. When burned its words
can still be read in the scraps. News stays news.
Even when someone wants it to disappear.
Reported that Daphne was happiest as a tree,
twenty feet and still growing. Not a hurtful thing.
Have I made it clear? Not so much as
a pilliwinks is permitted to enter here.

Now, Voyeur

We were arguing: Is all looking voyeuristic? Gazing isolates things. You mean separates you from them. What about all looking at paintings? This woman with one green breast. On a divan. Eve again, I said. Apple green. Earlier I'd said, Eve climbed the cyclone fence. Who wouldn't have? The room appears tiny and ill-kempt. Is she bleeding? Sheets look like egg white and she's the yolk. She has fallen onto the divan; she's broken. It's cruel. You shrug. Just look at what's there, I mean what's painted. *No story-telling.* But mood follows image, I said, even you can't escape that. We stare at the nipple. It's on the wall dangling like a shade-pull. Aha! see, it's like the window shade's left halfway up. That's no accident. We are caught being voyeurs, peeking through the window. Well, yes, you say, who wouldn't?

Old State Asylum: Two Photographs

I.

Wrought in the Victorian era,
the window's iron bars
form elongated diamonds.
Rosette disks hide the joints.

Its panes long gone,
a thick vine coiled round
the rusty grid till it too
gave up the ghost.
A white-grey decayed
vegetation still beards it,
as though it expired of old age

& not the effort, once
twisted inside, to get
back out.

II.

A lone metal bed
in a long-abandoned ward:
observe how time has had
its surreal way with it—

stretched it, bent it down &
out to a gigantic grin
above a thickly littered floor,

awful grin
that furnishes a room
where ruin, or a mind,
once wandered in.

Letter from Limbo

And should I
tell of the winged domicile
    beneath which course the passageways
that link us all
    like vascular cells?

It's no trap.
It will not clamp on a spring
    or snap toothed jaws. Careful as a
mom cat's carriage
    of kits in her mouth.

Windows with
not a single latch or lock—
    remember we were virtuous.
Still are. Halls bend
    to deposit us

at our friends'
and to our fond intentions.
    Invitations arrive as blue
butterflies, and
    it's rude to decline.

Privacy
is not a luxury here.
    Sentiment's an occupation.
No chimneys but
    the best carved mantles,

faux hearths to
help recall what that glow was.
    Hope hovers in the attic which
ladders barely
    reach and madness rules.

Shhhouldn't say:
my chamber's ceiling fan's an
    asterisk, under whose shadow
lie I, history's
    eternal footnote.

ASYLUM
SONG

"What do you call a group of ...?"

a *siege* of ~~herons~~ heredities
a *cloud* of ~~flies~~ lies
a *sloth* of ~~bears~~ forebears
a *game* of ~~swans~~ cons
a *labor* of ~~moles~~ millwrights
a *bevy* of ~~roes~~ woes
a *barren* of ~~mules~~ miscarriages
a *superfluity* of ~~nuns~~ wounds
a *pity* of ~~prisoners~~ immigrants
a *covert* of ~~coots~~ white coats
a *destruction* of ~~wild cats~~ maniacs
a *hover* of ~~trout~~ traumas
a *drift* of ~~quails~~ details
a *tiding* of ~~magpies~~ more lies
a *knot* of ~~toads~~ words
a *cowardice* of ~~curs~~ ours

Icebox

Cornered in the kitchen, my mother
    clutched the dishrag.
  My therapist had sent me on a mission
    to probe her, to wake
  the sleeping dogs who'd dozed so long
    they'd become the bones they dreamed about.
Well, you know, it was the Depression
    she'd often say as though that explained away
  every lapse. Mother eyed the refrigerator,
    kept trying to change the subject . . .

          (In a dream I climbed a steep staircase and
            found a room lined with black cabinets.

  So, your mother died in childbirth?
Um, it was complications . . . When? I pressed. *Oh,*
    a few months after (already the story I knew
      was beginning to shift)
    Who took care of you then?
Well, we had a house . . . Where was that?
          How did your father react?
          Who took care of the baby?

Depression.
Complications.

          (In the dream I'm shocked to discover
           a book on a table my mother has written.

What is it?

She was intently wiping the icebox, as she still called it.

What is this spot? she said, exasperated.

Back and forth the dishcloth went

round and round and round

Corrigenda
for "More Raw Data"

(*Placebo Effects*, 1997)

For "A woman dying in childbirth
in the twenties—one less
immigrant in Fishtown."

> Substitute *A woman dying post-partum
> in a state asylum—one less
> immigrant in Clifton Heights.*

For the heaviness of a secret, correct "a dull satchel of bricks"

> to *a full satchel of documents.*

Change "hidden, the way I heard it" to *written, the way I learned of it.*

After "The father, courting new women,
gave everything away."

> Add *My mother learned this:
> give nothing away.*

In place of "every word is another patch
of the motley...
habitation in which
I try to blend in"

> Insert *each microfiche is another patch
> of the story...
> information which
> I try to amend.*

The line "I ferreted these facts by stealth" should be footnoted as follows:

* census records, immigration records, ship manifests, certificates of birth, baptism, marriage, and death, hospital records.

To the "One theory" add a second:

The more answers you find, the more questions arise.

I wrote "If I'd been told it / the rest of the story / would follow:"

It follows ...

Portrait with Closed Eyes

She was the stain in the teacup
   that spread up toward the handle.
She was the handle that snapped
   off the hairbrush, and
She was the hairbrush he tossed
   onto the fire, and
She was the fire he carried
   each day in his pipe.

She was the pipe the bath water
   rode to the river, and
She was the river where they
   boarded the boat to limbo.
She was the limbo that held
   the secrets of acorns, and
She was the acorn that
   bruised his weary knees.

She was the knees that knocked
   beneath the oak table, and
She was the table where glasses
   were refilled till midnight.
She was the midnight that darkened
   the brow of the child,
Child who never felt safe indoors,
   who never felt safe outdoors.

She, the heaviest of doors, was the reason.
   She was their stain.

Asylum: Case No. 10518

(In beloved memory of Anna K., 1893–1927)

*

Case No. 10518

How Committed Dir. of Poor   *How Supported* Dir. of Poor

Clothing State

Age 34 yrs.

Nativity Czecho-Slovakia   *Time in U. S.* 14 yrs.

Economic Condition Dependent   *Environment* Rural

Occupation Wife of Mill Worker   *Religion* R. Catholic

Children Four

No. of Admissions First

Physical Condition on Admission Impaired

Result Died   {*Date* August 1st, 1927

Cause of Death Exhaustion from Mental Disease (Mania)

*

WHY DO YOU THINK SHE IS INSANE?

threatens violence to herself and family.
Bites and screams.

        Worried about child left in old cou

is unmanageable. Has to be restrained
                            broke out
into an attack of acute mania

tried to choke her baby
tried to be run over by the street car
tried to take a neighbors baby

required two or three people
      required three or four people to
      handle her

              worries about an illegiti

daughter whom she has not seen for 14 yrs.

Is in fear that someone is going to shoot her.

          it becomes necessary
          to restrain her.

*

A knot of waterfowl, a wisp of snipe

Admitted July 12th, 1927 at 9 a. M.   Bathed at: 9:30 a.M.

TENDENCIES: Suicidal   Yes

Condition of Person: (General Nutrition, Cleanliness, Vermin, etc)

General Nutrition good
Head and Body dirty
Weight not obtained
Height "   "

Skin: Bruises on arms and legs

RETURN THIS SLIP TO OFFICE

---

*

Adam's Anamnesis

(July 14, 1927)

Her husband recollected that her parents were born in Hungary.
That her mother and her father had died of old age.
He recollected that one of her two brothers had been killed in war.
He recollected No insane relatives.
 And thus it was recorded.

He recollected their four children—all normal deliveries.
He recalled that one child had died of "kidney trouble" at 2 years.
He said his wife was Always well.
He recollected she occasionally complained of headaches.
 And thus it was recorded.

He recollected no peculiar conduct until Monday, July 11th.
At which time she suddenly began to shriek, and rave, etc....
A doctor was sent for, who failed in giving her a hyperdermic [sic].
The next day she was sent to State Hospital.
 And thus it was recorded.

He recollected she was never in a hospital before;
has had no illnesses since he has known her.
He recalled that they'd been married 11 years.
Always well. Is what he recollected.
 And thus it was recorded.

*

A rag of colts, a clowder of cats

extremely destructive
of clothing, she burst out
of her camisole

to give an enema
required the assistance
of five nurses

in her menstrual cycle,
the flow is not profuse
there are no clots

will not stay in bed
pounds on the door, seems to be
in mental distress

when not under
an opiate
whirls most of the time

*

A chattering of choughs, a gaggle of geese

7-12-27   The patient admitted to Section 3
Speaks no English
      does not seem to know where she is going

          cries and mutters
          unintelligible phrases
          in her own language

Shows no understanding

      cries, shrieks
      pays no attention to anyone
      is abusive and dangerous
      to herself and others

Her tongue was coated
and her lips were dry

7-13-27   Pt became extremely noisy

      apparently does not understand
        English and her attention
      cannot be held sufficiently
      to converse with an interpreter

7-16-27   ...According to a Polish interpreter
she realizes she is in the hospital

      she will occasionally make remarks in Polish,
      "Close the door, or,
      Leave me alone."

7-17-27   Weeps without apparent cause.

*

A building of rooks (a rookery)

In hospitals they count by beds
     one   two   three
beds occupied   beds empty

> *(The state's first inpatient psychiatric facility*
> *had space for 2,983.)*

On July 12th, 1880, The State Lunatic Hospital's red-brick complex
   received its first patient, a woman,
     two & three   followed the next day
        546 by end of September . . .

And 47 years *to that day*   (no bells, no prize, no cake)
     to the now-named State Hospital of the Insane
     this one arrived on a stretcher
        in hand restraints that had swollen her wrists
   under the influence of morphine:
   "a well-developed and well nourished young woman"
     was given a bed bath
     was given a bed in
Ward D, Section 3
   and on the 13th it reached 93°
     and our patient would not   stay in bed.

> *(How many patients by then were housed in its*
> *stack-ventilated wards? The hospital was still*
> *some thirty years from its >4,500 peak capacity.)*

Three   four   five   days later
      patient continued to be   disturbed
      preferred to lie on the floor   resisted
      attempts to place her   on the bed
          "may be due to the excessively hot weather"

> *(Old frames of cot-like institutional beds,*
> *metal bars at foot and head,*
> *leant against walls, sagged, left*
> *behind, here and there along*
> *abandoned halls. Was this her bed*
> *or some better kind?)*

On July 29th she was "growing weaker"
      sleeping most of the time. It was 90°
and the one who'd arrived by ambulance
      took up the bed in Ward D
      one
           two
               three
weeks, and cooler it was on the day she
expired, cooler with less than an inch of rain
      and the bed was turned over again, again . . .

> *(By the early 1970s*
> *Norristown State Hospital's*
> *bed census had begun*
> *to drop significantly.*
> *Just under 400 beds recently.)*

*

A watch of nightingales

(7-17-27)

Slept none during the night; extremely noisy

Pulse rapid and weak.

> Given: camphorated oil
> Digitalen
> morphine
> Atropin
> Sponge treatment during the night.

This morning was more quiet
and somewhat clearer mentally.

> Took Epsom salts ½ oz

Visited by the priest.

*

An interlude, in which Anna drifts

somewhere mid-Atlantic, 1913
               the sun bullies, the chop batters
and she one of the horde aboard the *S.S. Patricia*
       feels lost between two ports
               Hamburg   &   New York
she, having left her known world—
       father, mother, brother, babe (*had she a babe to leave?*)
at sea,
           never to see   again   again
               (*if you carry a secret, will it become a disease?*)

Days afloat blurred into nights into days,
               November into December,
and her brow faced west   fleeing what?
                   what toward?
with thirty-five dollars in her pocket, or hem
       or brim of a hat (*had she even a hat?*)
Had she even one friend?
    Was Sofia her lean-on whisper-to steerage sister? She also
    twenty, from the same town, the name below hers on the manifest.
    Both entered "Slovak" "dom"(estic), a species like flies

                       waiting to land
two lives   suspended between   two lives
emigrant   immigrant
She was green and
       she was green
       (*if you arrive with a secret, will you always be a mystery?*)

Now here she was adrift again

again at sea, another three-week fever-dream

dock   to   dock

tossed

and lost

betwixt   between

*

A mute of hares

From July 19th to 24th, a gap in the patient's log.
There's no extra space, nothing looks redacted
or erased. Did the recording nurse
go on vacation? Was the file misplaced?
Was our patient's status so stationary
nothing merited remark?

> *All we uncover for these 6 days*
> *is local weather:*
> > *highs ranged from 74 to 86,*
> > *upper 60s for the lows.*
> *Some days it rained*
> *the record shows.*

When the log resumes 7-25
    patient has been quiet . . . treatment
    has been continued.

In addition, this: dated July 26th, a mere 4 × 5 inch slip of paper
    with one sentence grants permission
to cut the hair of Anna K.
        believing it to be for
        the betterment of her health.
            Someone neatly signed her husband Adam's name.
            Beside the signature is writ
            per the name of their daughter
            the ten-year-old daughter
            "per" her. Why her?
            Why witness for her father?
            Was she visiting there?

There were only five days left.

Did they ever cut the hair?

*

A parliament of owls, a shrewdness of apes

(7-25-27)

Patient's papers read at staff today
(10 Drs. present):
Is in a state of mania and can not be seen
by the staff.
Is too greatly disturbed
to have any strangers
brought to her room.

Has been restrained and
under narcotics since admission

The staff agreed to the diagnosis
Manic Depressive Psychoses (Manic type).

*

A flight of swallows

Spiritus Frumenti, *the spirit of the grain,*
was "bottled in bond" during prohibition,
sold by prescription and specifically marked
"For Medicinal Purposes Only"

> syn. *alcohol, whiskey, corn, distill, drink, liquor, bourbon,*

Brands like Antique and Four Roses,
100 Proof, claimed "aged in wood,"
"topmost class," and for physician permittees,
"unexcelled for Medicinal Use"

e.g., 7-16-27   Patient is receiving egg nog with Spiritus
Frumenti.

> syn. *rye, booze, poteen, moonshine,*

e.g., 7-18-27   She takes liquid nourishment very well,
particularly egg nog with Spts. of Frumenti,
which she seems to relish as though she were
accustom [*sic*] to the use of same.

> syn. *hooch, rotgut, mountain dew,*

e.g., 8-1-27   Patient has been given stimulated treatment
. . . Digitalan alternating with Spts. of
Frumenti, and hot salt solution by bowel
. . . She did not respond well to this
treatment but grew progressively weaker
and died at 8:55 A.M., apparently from
exhaustion.

> *spirits, white lightning, usque-baugh*—lit. *water of life*

*

A descent of woodpeckers, a communion of saints

7-12   *Knock. Knock.*
                    Who's at the Asylum gate?

It's case number 10518,
accompanied by her husband and an officer
and neighbors, all in an excited state
(except Anna, due to the opiate).

7-13   *Knock. Knock.*
                    Who's there?

It's Anna herself, pounding on the door.
(What do you think she's doing that for?)

7-15   *Knock. Knock.*
                    Who is it?

It's the priest; first visit.

7-16   *Knock. Knock.*
                    Tell me, who?

A "Polish interpreter" (she knows Czech too?)

7-17   *Knock. Knock.*
                    Who's here to see our patient?

Some relatives and the priest are present,
and Anna's reported in "a state of excitement"
although still considered suffering depression
and the next day deemed "inaccessible
for satisfactory examination."

7-25   *Knock. Knock.*
                    Go away! Go away.

As we said, Anna K. is too greatly disturbed
to have strangers brought in today.

7-29   *Knock. Knock.*
                    Who's there?

Her relatives seek her, but Anna's much weaker.

7-30   *Knock. Knock.*
                    Who visits?

Her friends, and the priest (he's faithful at least).

8-1   *Knock. Knock. Knock.*
                    It's not yet 9 o'clock,
                    who calls for our sad case?

'Tis death.
With three in white to witness:
Zella and Nellie and Grace.

                    *

Post Mortem

Who killed Anna K.?

Not I, said Belladonna of the nightshade family.
    I supply atropine to dilate pupils, anesthetize.
    It's true I can produce rapid heart rate,
    but I'm an antidote to poisoning with morphine.
    Only overdose will cause coma, convulsions,
    delirium. Look, I prevent cardiac slowing—
    it surely was not me!

Not I, said the Camphor Tree. I produce cooling.
    I've been given for minor heart symptoms,
    fatigue. In the 1800s I was used to *treat* mania.
    In larger quantities, yes, I'm poisonous—
    seizures, confusion, irritability ... yes, yes,
    the FDA banned *camphorated oil* in 1980.
    But in this case I was a minor player.

Not I, said Foxglove, as the source of Digitalan
    I've been used for heart conditions
    since the 18th century. I help control heart rate,
    I'm approved for failing hearts. It's a fact
    my whole plant's toxic, called Dead Man's Bells,
    Witches' Gloves. Too much of me brings nausea,
    convulsions, disturbances of vision, well, well, maybe
    safety concerns, but history's on my side—you
    can't pin this on me.

Not I, said the Grain, why are you after me again?
I was given as a stimulant, and she liked me.
I was one of her few friends. That I should not
have been given along with morphine, well,
that was no fault of mine. I'm perfectly legal now.
Not guilty. Leave me be!

Not I, said the Poppy. I've been called God's Own Medicine
for all the suffering I've relieved. There's good reason
I am named for Morpheus, the god of dreams.
A soul could do worse than rest in my golden arms.

... send thy angels to conduct her to a place of refreshment, light, and peace. Amen.

Asylum Song

Who'll sing a psalm? "I," said the thrush,
"As I sit in a bush. I'll sing a psalm."

Do you remember your old friend Palimpsest?
Do you recollect your admittance?
O immigrant, your final journey and stop.
Let us scrape down to under-layers,
each color revealing an older brighter one.
Who cut out this window for a vista?
Who put in your hand a heart-shaped stone?
How to soften so sad a song?

We live in boxes, this your last.
Take the thin dry hand of benevolence.
Baby step, scissors step, umbrella step—
down the long forgiving corridor
you went, now a chipped and sunlit ruin.
Where's the flower-bearing goddess,
and twisted key deft as a skeleton?
How to unlock the past's sad song?

From the chair where you found rest,
you can spy far out in the distance
small specks toward the mountaintop:
Cousins, husband, son, daughters,
each hand linking to other ones.
So this is how you will persist.
Now a voice at your shoulder beckons
        Build a world of beauty, live in it.
You won't have long, you don't have long.

By Way of Farewell

Tell me, my long lost grandmother,
Why you left all and crossed over the water.
　　　—It was hope, alas.

Tell me, my missing grandmother,
Why did you marry one so much older?
　　　—It was hope, alas.

　　　Granddaughter, you've never known Hunger,
　　　What it gnawed in me when I was younger
　　　　　—It was hope, alas.

O tell me, grandmother forlorn,
What you felt when each child was born.
　　　—It was hope, alas.

Grandmother, that day your last summer,
Why did you put your babe in danger?
　　　—I'd lost hope, alack.

Poor grandmother, what made you crack
And jump out on the streetcar track?
　　　—I'd lost hope, alack.

　　　Please, granddaughter, do not blame or judge me
　　　For leaving your mother abruptly
　　　　　—I'd lost hope, alack.

O tell me, my manic grandmother,
Why your young heart grew weaker and weaker?
　　　—It was hope, alas. A lack.

HOLDING

Letter from Limbo

If granted reprieve, some of us argue
We'd refuse to leave. Isn't this the best
Of circumstances? How have happiness
Without hope? How hope without chance of rescue?
To have all resolved must bring misery.
How then can hopeless heaven offer bliss?
Anticipation's pleasures would be missed—
A hole in sheer joy's fabric for eternity.

Others claim that hope's a garment woven
Only to be worn in time; immortal
Souls cast it off as a bird in molt will
Shed old colors. But I choose expectancy—
Immersion in this indefinite haven's
My sweet sabbatical under the sea.

Abelia

Beneath the window, bees are dizzy with delight
    among the abelia. They hover
amid the perfumed surround, plunge their heads

like party-goners under lampshades then
    back away, change flowers, and re-dance.
Fear not, child. They care nothing for you.

And you are safe behind the screen
    in the cooler dining room. For this occasion
even your father endures a pink conical birthday hat.

Elastic presses the flesh of each one's chin.
    The whole family sings off-key. For you,
the streamers, candles, melting ice cream.

Mother bends close to help you slice
    the cake-mix cake. Later you watch
your grandmother reapply the lips her tea

took away, speechless before such intimacy.
    It is silent again in the house.
The bees drone as one, faintly, faintly

and you alone are still young enough
    to hear them.

The Talk

Father rode behind the wheel,
    where he seemed most at home,
    driving to Mass or school or
less dreadful, to the deli or drugstore—

errands for the one who lay on the couch
    that day or stayed in bed
    stymied by her hopeless hair,
frequent excuse why she couldn't go out.

With his habitual periphrasis
    he turned toward me to mildly scold,
    Try not to upset your mother,
she had a very unhappy childhood.

Or maybe he said *Be nice to her,*
    but the words glanced off the same.
    I was young. I thought *I* was having one—
pent-up, pimply, misunderstood.

How much did he withhold
    about what she'd witnessed then?
    She had lost her mother at ten.
That I was told. Did he know

of the asylum—what happened
    next, was never mentioned?
    I sensed secrets were being held,
heard the hush round certain names,

but it all swirled too remote to matter
    to me, terrible daughter that I was
    (it's only now I feel the shame),
I kept on fighting with my mother.

Letter from Limbo

It's not what you surmise, this abode, this abiding
is no state for those with habits of impedance,
those unable to complete.

Homes where boxes stay unpacked or walls part-painted,
a room where thin pattern tissue remains pinned to
fabric never finished into

dress (despite her fondness for those small rose roses
on black background, longed-for pleats of Juliet sleeves
left unstitched ... but I digress)—

Earth-work survives messy process, half that/half this.
To sustain our decommissioned domain demands
constant imagining,

each *me* each moment keeping one piece, holding on.
That's how we're holding up.

Good Nothing and Good Night

Whenever I pass a house under construction—open
frame squared on its foundation—I'm thrown back

to my first adult embrace, to a bitter January day,
old snow tattering the mounds around the site, drum

echo of our boots on raw planks, evening's first grays
pouring through the unclosed roof, had we paused

to look up or out. Trespassing, which carried its own
modest thrill (though no one cared about these

nascent suburban properties), we stood chilled at
the brink of fourteen, as I calculate now, yet how

serious I felt, and sincerely wooed, while sensing
the way the world was already closing in on us

as those walls soon would to complete a space
deemed inhabitable, but that dusk our mouths

nearly froze together, our coats bulky, our breaths
mist, and the framed-out doorway meant

little to us who walked through walls at will
content with the nothing we stepped

out to and the nowhere we were headed.

Pathmark (1978)

The enormous Pathmark Supermart was set alone
up a long hill, requiring acceleration of my Malibu
to arrive in a parking lot of stadium dimensions.
What expectations it must have been built on and
OPEN "24/7" though that phrase was not yet in use.
I'd stop in the off-off hours to cruise its wide empty aisles
under the buzz of commercial fluorescence
while the sparse nightshift swept tile and restocked.
Because I was bulimic then, I had peanut butter, jelly,
crackers, cookies, and pints of coffee ice cream
barely covering the bottom of my family-sized cart.
Once in the daytime I'd run into someone here
I was trying to avoid for the rest of my life, so the only
solution as I saw it was to shop late.
                              As I exited
goose-armed from the overkill AC, suburbia's
August air swathed me like a damp shawl.
Crickets pulsed like mad.
A half-moon tilted toward the towering light posts.
I paused to take in the oddness of that lot
raised high amid the universe. Me in it improbable, near absurd.
What felt impending seemed benign
though I was alone in a way I was still getting used to.
I set my bag of groceries on the backseat, locked doors
as I'd been taught, popped in an 8-track for the drive.
And nothing else happened.
My life was as ahead of me as it was behind.
Be-lieve ... believe in ... mys—ter—y ...
David Byrne urged, like a prayer, I joined in.

A Seated Figure

Who was it that danced sitting down? you asked. The Copasetics, I said, the famous chair tap-dance. It's harder than dancing upright. If you can dance in a chair, you can dance anywhere. We were facing the blue figure in the blue box. Seated on no visible chair. It was erased, you said, but the figure stays in place, like pulling the rug out from someone. Or the tablecloth from under the place settings, I said. Or, or . . . you stopped. Death pulls the chair out from under us. Yes, I said, but he does look like he's dancing a jolly jig. There's a jag of red on his collar, a flare of color on his hand. The other arm juts out, almost like *swing your partner*. No (you were feeling dire), this is the last dance this man is doing, in the dark room of the cold universe. Death's our final unshirkable partner. That I had to admit. Shave and a lament, two bits? Not so fast, you said, taking my arm and easing me out of the room.

Dream of X

A person who has entered your body
never entirely exits.

The body's brain is full of doors on trick hinges.
Some push in, some push out.

Some only dreams can break down, bring back.
Dream knows the necessity of artifice, disguise,

knows how two may briefly lock eyes:
Bonnie looks at Clyde, Clyde at Bonnie.

Tune up the fiddle, tighten the bow.
The aftermath of two minus one minus one—

Clyde's a fog on the mountain,
and Bonnie's mist over the sea . . .

In memoriam W. E. W.

Dear empty coat,

The black doorway was always there
and it didn't matter what sort of chair
you set in front of it. Long ago you'd
turned a key with your nimble foot, you
unscrewed the door itself from its jamb,
and so the abyss waited. Stood by like
a butler, a fucking butler, a cosmic joke
you came to appreciate by increments.
It was there in your moaning mouth
beyond your tombstone teeth.
It was there when you walked the dog,
beneath the grate you passed over, and
didn't he stop to gather in for both your sakes
its incriminating scents, and didn't your
two shadows walk ever after nearer than
even your chain-linked bodies?

One moment you were half-dissolving
in a little lion tamer's chair or retching
into a cracked sink or writhing in bed,
flesh spotted like rotting fruit.
Botched cruel life was still life.
You woke up each morning a wonder.
Next you were curled at the threshold
like one rough-treated but treated,
we needed to believe, holding on or pinned.
When did your foot slip over dragging
its leg, and how then were we looking at the

void, last mouth you'd apparently fallen out into?
Exit flesh. Feat or ascent or—
A rush of oily cold air twisted up our faces.
Let words stay your world stains—*refuse to transfigure.*

In memoriam J. W.

Our Skeleton

Arrived with the sound
of scuttling paper
single file
across the floor

Aha! said one
Uh huh, said another   *I have a bone to pick with you,*
                                          Anti said on the phone

Smelled of camphor
from a chest of old fleece,
a sickening sweet
reek underneath

Oh no, I said
Whaddya know! said another   *Hush,* Anti said, *won't you*
                                          let it rot in peace

Wobbled like a marionette
on its rigging
lurching about
a makeshift stage

I wonder if…, said one
We might have guessed, said another   *You're dead wrong!* Anti said,
                                          why don't you stop digging

Began to answer queries
with a nod or a knock—
despite bare bones we found
some resemblance

That explains … one began

Now I see, said another   *Stop prying,* Anti pled, *shut*
                                              the door and set the lock!

But we'd come to love our skeleton far too much to turn back

The Ghost Baby

tugged at my sleeve in the bar (of all places!).
I didn't want to pay attention.
Listen, you were the one sent to listen.
I'll tell you where I was conceived, a cottage on the rocks,
a lake, lots of trees. A dapper foursome
they were then, happy as chipmunks in Eden.
I didn't want to pay attention.

I knew pictures in an album:
Mother's head disappearing in the fog.
Father smart in his fedora, two-toned brogues.
Two neat children in hand-stitched clothes.
You've seen the photo then when
father holds mother from the brink.
I didn't want to see, I said. I didn't want—

To think! How he grips her shoulders.
It was not long after the war. Children
were trying to return to earth, I was among them,
the ghost child said. *Listen . . . p a y a t t e n t i o n . . .*
Only a wayward wind. What does it matter?
Attention dims. Speculation fades.
Superstition, I said. Everyone knows it:
a ghost is only a gust of lost wind.

Letter from Limbo

It's not that things never change here—
it's the pace of the change. Imagine a bell
that takes centuries to complete its ring,
a slow motion arc well beyond leaden,

that's the pace of the change. Imagine a bell,
the infinitesimal motions of the clapper,
a slow motion arc well beyond leaden,
and you might start to feel the pull and drag

on the infinitesimal motions of its clapper.
Become aware of the bell's confines,
and you might start to feel the pull and drag
of the borderlines within which change can occur.

Become aware the bell's confines are
like the sacred space inside any circumference,
the boundaries within which change will occur
filled with the hush of ecstatic anticipation

like any sacred space inside a circumference.
We're in a kinetic process, but it won't be rushed,
filled with the hush of ecstatic anticipation.
True, alteration here is gradual and hemmed by margins.

We're in a kinetic process that won't be rushed—
seasons of damp thaw, raw heat, chilled hibernation—
true alteration here is gradual and hemmed by margins
but nevertheless we've the security of repetition:

seasons of damp thaw, raw heat, chilled hibernation
that take centuries to complete gyring
but nevertheless weave the security of repetition.
It's not that things never change here.

"Mere" Hypotheses

Limbo is enduring.

Limbo became overpopulated.

Limbo was an overlooked typo.

Limbo possessed negative capability.

Limbo is an invisible city.

Ambiguity and Obscurity spawned Limbo.

Limbo persists on the head of a nail.

Limbo is genderless.

Limbo cannot be cured.

Limbo was a liturgical accident.

Limbo is hell to the most delicate.

There are no heroes in Limbo.

Limbo is a thorn in the pope's side.

Limbo is a colonized community.

Because it does not exist, Limbo was invented.

Limbo is a junkyard dogma.

Limbo is a buoyant mystery.

Limbo will always be prone to static.

Limbo is unbecoming.

When I Think

about how naive I was though never
admitting it, how badly I chose early on
spending my affections carelessly as
spare change then making quick getaways
igniting the bridges— or when I think of the time
wasted brooding and stewing, my heart a sort of
crock pot simmering bitterness, it's good to be
grown up at last with boxes of journals I'm unlikely
to get back to and albums of photos as a very
selective mnemonic aid as though most of life
had been a string of holidays, reunions, bright
birthday parties, and not the dreary Mondays,
Friday nights watching old black & white movies,
hands ink-stained from the newspaper, waits
at the post office, subway, trips to the drugstore,
thousands of bowls of cereal, pots of soup— And
when I think of all those I went to school with,
worked alongside, ate with, taught, those I will not
ever see again due to the odd cruel way time
shakes us and scatters us and never recombines
us even perhaps someone I was married to, even
him, and those I failed or let down or otherwise
proved myself a disappointment to, and those I will
never share the same time and place with, we will never
coincide, and that's a shame but also reassuring
because how much are we capable of accumulating,
of absorbing, of holding, for already I try to grasp
one thing only to feel another slip away to make room,
a musical chairs of the mind and who keeps taking

a chair away— so that when I think of the finite
it seems the most profound fact, the boundaries
of minutes, years, borders of gardens and countries,
frame of the painting, edge of the screen, that one
chair left though it has the softest fabric, high back,
cushions to nod right off in until the music stops.

Letter from Limbo

Like smoke in a jar, rumors circulate
    about a denizen called back,
or up. I've never seen one pack,
    never observed an "exit"
although occasionally a greenish
    (as I remember green) cone
of queasy light will surround one
    who will then nearly vanish
or diminish in a way—since
    everything occurs here all at once
(so please excuse my frequent
    gaffs of tense)—I can't convey
or offer evidence except, as I say,
    rumors of clandestine calls for volunteers.
But such green could be an aura
    that precedes arrival. I'm sure you
understand our dilemma, our collective
    black-out of comings & goings.
How came I here? Did I *appear*?
    I only know I live.

Around Her

My mother is so old her sixty-year
marriage disappears in the rear-view mirror.
Her hair has passed through three shades of white.
Her blue eyes turn still bluer as though sky or
some deeper heaven loomed in her sights.
So old she doesn't remember the child
she had who, tortured by bullies, came tearing
through the backyard, sobbed for broke in her arms.
Doesn't remember braiding over and over
her daughters' hair. She can't remember her
houses, her clotheslines, how she loved the smell
of air-dried sheets. Now strangers come to change
her sheets. Most days she forgets to get dressed.

My sister talks her out of her stained robe by bringing a replacement
then whisking the other away to wash. Hereafter, mother will switch
from pink to mint green like a traffic light in Candyland.

My mother is so old the past has closed
behind her like massive cathedral doors.
The present is the stream of light that pours
between them. Don't ask if she can recall
whose eyes look out from photos around her.
We are all surrounded, and *beloveds* names
well enough. She's been burning so long on
this earth that time circles her like a frame
of smoke. When I reach through it for a hug,
we embrace like those who part before an
arduous journey. Will we two meet again?
Her eyes already focused far away,
she labors to catch the last words I say.

Letter from Limbo

You ask what glories we have access to, being
"excluded from the beatific vision" as defined.

Best is the firmament—barred from heaven
but not the heavens, which open for us

like a colossal jewelry box. I wish I could
show you the odd-pitched graduated ladders

that lift us to great heights of star-gazery.
Up and down we traverse, birdlike in big-

sleeved scholar's gowns, tailored to trap
breezes and bear us up (we can climb

only half as far without them). To see
our billowing citizenry hung high amid

the heavens, some with telescopes, some with
maps and charts, others with sets of paint,

is to witness a form of rapture, one
in which no body need be left behind.

If not all astronomers, or amateurs at best,
we're all admirers who take our profoundest

pleasure in planets and comets, in moons
and meteor showers, in galactic treasures so

phenomenal I'm not permitted to describe them,
except to say, they're far beyond what satellites

or spaceships could offer, which is to say,
we're so much more than clothed and fed.

Notes

Poems on pages 8, 22, 66, and 68 make reference to various paintings by Francis Bacon.

Asylum Song: Much of this section consists of found material.

The poem "What do you call a group of ...?" is drawn from the Oxford Dictionaries Online.

The full text of "More Raw Data" can be found on pages 45-48 of my collection *Placebo Effects* (Norton, 1997).

The 1927 case papers for Anna K. were released to my family from Norristown State Hospital in Pennsylvania. I have tried to be true to the facts of that record and let it speak for itself. Information about the history and current status of the hospital was obtained from their website. Special thanks to Carol Clayton for her fruitful and dedicated detective work.

The weather information was taken from the records of the Franklin Institute of Philadelphia. Information about Anna's immigration was taken from the Ellis Island archives. Additional documentation was obtained from http://www.rootsweb.ancestry.com/~asylums as well as other sites devoted to the history of asylums in the United States.

Drug and medicinal whisky information was drawn from various online encyclopedias and sites; it is not intended to be anything but a poetic interpretation of historic practice.

"By Way of Farewell" is based on 13th-century Galician forms.

"When I Think" is written after Robert Creeley's poem of the same title.

Acknowledgments

Thank you to the editors of the following publications, where these poems first appeared, some in earlier incarnations:

American Arts Quarterly: "In Preparation," "The Room and the View"
American Literary Review: "Abelia," "Letter from Limbo [Like smoke]"
Calibanonline: "'Mere' Hypotheses"
Cave Wall: "Pathmark (1978)"
Cerise Press: "A Day in Lavender"
Court Green: "Dream of X," "The Ghost Baby," "Now, Voyeur"
Harvard Review: "Folk Art Portraits of the 1700s"
Hotel Amerika: "Dear empty coat," "Letter from Limbo [If granted reprieve]," "Letter from Limbo [It's not that things]"
I-70 Review: "The Talk"
Manhattan Review: "Letter from Limbo [If you'd stop to]," "Letter from Limbo [You ask what glories]," "Yet"
New Letters: "Letter from Limbo [If it proves possible]," "A Seated Figure"
Pool: "Letter from Limbo [It's not what you surmise]"
Ploughshares: "Fifteen Views of a Christening Gown," "Portrait with Closed Eyes"
Roger: "When I Think"
Saranac Review: "Asylum Song," "Letter from Limbo [How often our locale]," "Letter from Limbo [Now that our version]"
Southern Poetry Review: "Good Nothing and Good Night," "Letter from Limbo [It can be claimed]"
Spoon River Poetry Review: "Letter from Limbo [Let this missive assure]"
Stonecoast Review: "Crossing"

A special thank you to the Dana Awards, which gave five of the "*Letter from Limbo*" poems first prize for poetry, and to the editors of *Hotel Amerika* and *I-70 Review* for Pushcart nominations. Affection and gratitude to sustaining friends and readers Cynthia Atkins, Teresa Carson, Judith Harris, Susan Thomas, Sarah White, and Baron Wormser. Deep appreciation to Joan Cusack Handler for keeping an open ear, heart, and door. Love and thanks to my family for letting me be the storyteller.

CavanKerry's Mission

CavanKerry Press is committed to expanding the reach of poetry to a general readership by publishing poets whose works explore the emotional and psychological landscapes of everyday life.

Other Books in the Notable Voices Series